Your Spiritual Child

Your
Spiritual
Child

Barbara Milicevic

DeVorss & Company
Box 550 – Marina del Rey – California 90294

ISBN: 0-87516-528-1
Library of Congress Card Catalog Number: 83-72945

Printed in the United States of America

Third Printing, 1989

I acknowledge with love and appreciation the co-operation and patience of my daughters, Tiffany and Bria, in posing for the yoga exercise pictures for Chapter 8 of this book.

B. R. M.

Author's Note: In examples used to illustrate principles, I have alternated gender references, rather than using he/she repeatedly.

CONTENTS

Introduction

Introduction

"When were you born?"

"Born?" the four year old replied indignantly. "I *wasn't* born."

"Where did you learn to play piano?" inquired the young man of the child at the piano bench, who was picking out an enchanting melody.

"I didn't learn. I just know."

"Mother, I feel like everything is a dream. And I feel there's someone watching us, waiting for us to wake up."

These are portions of actual conversations with some of our planet's gifted scholars—our children. Their giftedness is due to a purity of consciousness and yet uncluttered intuitive ability.

A truly intelligent adult will have the awareness to recognize this faculty and approach its unfoldment with enthusiastic respect.

It has been said there's a New Age dawning with the advent of the millennium. With this New Age many individuals are experiencing an awakening of the Self (the higher consciousness Self) and a perception of others as beings more complex than just the physical personality. It's an awakening to a new attitude of tolerance and understanding—a sense of unity, oneness.

This New Age brings a golden opportunity, an exciting adventure for you, as a parent, teacher or guardian, now. And it doesn't result from any high priced seminar, or expensive series of cassettes or in a secret meditation technique. There is a special excitement you can experience through recognizing and bringing forth the divine wisdom and radiance of your child.

With this awareness and hope for a better future many parents wonder, "How can I effectively guide my child to fully express his highest potential? And how do I best prepare him not only to deal with the world, but to be (not become, but *be*) a 'master of his environment'?"

As a guardian of today's child, you may feel you're facing a challenge you have not encountered before. Meeting the needs of your child, living in our fast-paced culture, is an awesome responsibility, indeed. It can appear an overwhelming and often discouraging task. You may have a vague feeling you could be doing more for your child, but are not sure how to go about it.

It is a natural instinct with many parents to want to protect their spiritually sensitive, naturally gifted child from the technological, material-minded world. This is understandable, but unrealistic.

The job that needs to be done is this. Assist your child to relate objectively to, and master, depressing negative situations while maintaining his higher consciousness. This is the noblest undertaking you can embark on. The obstacles your child will confront and move beyond are more complex and decadent than they have ever been; but at the same time, the heights can be loftier.

This book, if read with an open mind and heart, will help you to do two things. First, it can offer principles to help *you* seize control of your life by showing how our attitudes create our world around us. And, second, it will assist you in guiding your child toward self-mastery.

CHAPTER 1

Mastery

OUR INHERENT TRANSCENDENT NATURE

There never was a time you didn't exist! You have always been and always *will be*!! Feel the significance of this statement of truth.

You are in a naturally pure, inherent state of grace —in total communication with all secrets of the Universe. It is this state that you experience intermittently through your life when you inexplicably know answers—but don't know how it is you know them. Inventors and great thinkers through the ages have experienced this same state or feeling when they made historical discoveries. You are no different than they. It is our thoughts that we are average that keep us average.

All young children naturally experience this level of awareness. The development of it, however, depends on the environment—especially the thoughts and feelings of the parent(s). This fertile potential requires sensitive guidance. These little ones, a seeming contradiction of naive wisdom and vulnerability, can be emotionally crushed like hollow egg shells with one ill-thought statement or glance.

In teaching your child to expand his capacities you may confront blockages within yourself. You may feel a need to reassess your own awareness, to

1

get clear on your own attitudes toward life. Previous references you've used in relating to the world may seem stagnant and rigid.

Most of our difficulties are caused by a feeling that we are helpless in dealing with the world— that negative forces such as disease, inflation, sickness, war, and so forth, have us cornered. We often feel, yet are reluctant to admit, that we, too, are like dependent frightened children.

Encouraging your child to expresss his creative ideas in an unlimited way may force you to realize just how much you have allowed yourself to be limited. We expect and hope for our children to "go for it," and we reluctantly hold back on our own secret goals. You may discover your own latent wisdom has long been suppressed for the sake of conforming to others' expectations!

Children are strongly aware of many truths that adults need to be reminded of or taught—things we, too, once sensed.

SOCIAL ACCEPTANCE OF
SPIRITUAL AWARENESS

One encouraging note that has recently promoted social acceptance of the power of spiritual awareness is the scientific community's open-minded approach and empirical testing of the non-visible worlds, which many children are effortlessly aware of.

Clinical regressive hypnosis indicates the existence of an "essence" beyond physical man, an intelligence some call the "soul." This consciousness or essence can be traced back to the gestation period in the mother's womb and even before. The thoughts recorded during hypnosis were those of totally aware beings.

Because most people won't accept esoteric ideas until there is scientific documentation in its favor, it is a giant step forward for mankind that scientific perceptions have broadened about the eternal and non-physical nature of the universe. Now, more and more, the individual has the confidence to view his *own* nature as limitless and expansive, a thought he only wondered about before.

PRINCIPLES OF CREATING OUR OWN WORLD

It is an established fact that matter is *not solid*, but is *fluent energy*. Molecules vibrate quickly as in clouds or slowly as in wood, metal, or your physical body. What is even more amazing is at close examination these atoms themselves are made up of parts that disappear and reappear as they revolve around each other! So this is another aspect of our multi-dimensional ''beingness.'' We truly don't ''go'' anywhere, but we *are* physically ever-changing and limitless—existing in several dimensions at the same time!

These other dimensions, the invisible part of our existence, are not off in space somewhere else, but are right here, permeating our physical, three-dimensional world. Light, sound and temperature can fill a room at the same time because they are different qualities or vibrations of one Life Force or energy.

All life vibrates from the center outward. This can be seen from the rings of a tree, the spiraling of a galaxy. Even the evolution of the brain began with the core at the top of the spinal column; through the centuries, brain tissue developed around it to its present-day size, like the pearl around the grain of sand.

Masterpieces of today, from expansion bridges to great novels, began with the tiny spark of an idea.

It's the same with our daily experiences. Spiritual teacher Ernest Holmes states that all reality in this dimension is a result of seed ideas: our thoughts, our emotions and our goals. *These* are the finer, nontactile dimensions. And this is the creative process: *thought* (or an idea) coupled with *feeling* (emotion) moves into *form* (manifestation).

So what we are feeling and thinking comes into being in our environment. Our uncontrolled negative thoughts and feelings (about ourselves and others) result in daily frustrations, illnesses, debts, diseases and so-called accidents. There are really no accidents. We create everything with our harmonious or discordant thoughts and feelings.

We've all experienced how a day can start off wrong and get worse and worse, snowballing into one horrible event after another. We dwell on a negative experience and, in so doing, draw another one to us. Because where the attention is, the experience or event will follow.

We are constantly creating our experiences just as surely as we are thinking, but we do so *unconsciously*. We often "turn over the controls" to others around us who do our thinking for us with all kinds of negative suggestions. So why not be consciously creating? Ralph Waldo Emerson said that a man is what he thinks all day.

Realizing this, is step one. The difficulty that often follows is setting our thinking free, changing our attitudes and breaking away from the mass-consciousness programming we often received in childhood. From early on, we've been conditioned that we get colds in the winter, get cancer because one in three gets it, and suffer financial difficulty because the nation is in the throes of a recession.

This is hogwash. It is not the truth about you, your child or any of us.

When the Truth of our Being *is* realized—we experience prosperity, health, contentment, wisdom and the expression of total awareness. Newborns have this awareness until negative thoughts from their environment tell them differently.

To break free of negative conditioning, we must continually affirm the Truth of our Being, which is all things positive and harmonious—total health, orderly finances, relationships based on mutual respect, and happy, intelligent children. To experience anything else would be a "lie" about our destiny and would be an indication that our attitude (our thoughts and feelings) needs cleansing.

By rejecting, not listening to, the fearful thoughts of others concerning inflation, sickness, sorrow or death—they are robbed of their power. These things will not become a part of our lives.

Instead, joyously acknowledge the eternal, abundant nature of the true Self within. Realize that we are all masters of our environments.

GUIDING YOUR CHILD THROUGH TODAY'S CHALLENGES

Creative energy flows impersonally through each of us as a distributing center. It is our choice how to express it. This is the meaning of the biblical reference to free will.

When you and your child function at a high level of expression, wisdom and prosperity, health and happiness will flow into your lives, your community and the world. The power of this inner tranquility will radiate from you outward through the universe.

An awareness and sensitivity to the multi-dimensional reality at the core of your Being is the foundation of true mastery. This mastery is total awareness of and *control* over your moment-to-moment thoughts and feelings.

Children have a natural "feel" for living in and for the moment. They argue with a little playmate one minute and are best friends the next. They move from one experience to the next in joyful trust, when not taught otherwise. Encouraging children to develop their natural gift of spiritual confidence while learning to become more like them is really the key to successful living. "Unless ye become as little children, ye will not enter the kingdom" refers to adopting a childlike attitude of trust, free of anxiety, guilt and fear.

Your child initially has a natural awareness of the creative process and views the world in a beautifully holistic way. His "all-knowingness" includes perceptions of interdimensional entities (spaceships, elves, gnomes, faeries and spirits), seeing or feeling electromagnetic life force emanations (auras and telepathy) and tapping into experiences of other time periods and cultures: past, present, or future (time/space travel).

The degree to which your child can successfully

link his superconscious "all-knowingness" with conscious day-to-day awareness can be greatly enhanced through your sensitive guidance.

A little brown-eyed three-year-old sat at the dinner table one evening and told her amazed family about the time she lived "long time ago in another house," how her present mother was then her grandmother with "long gray hair in a ponytail down her back" and how the grandfather had died so the gramma lived with them. After several other details were related she matter-of-factly dropped the story and asked for another piece of bread.

The family did not discredit her story with snickers or with doubtful thoughts about it. This would have destroyed her confidence in her own experience.

When spontaneous outbursts of psychic perception such as this are handled more often with a matter-of-fact attitude—that is, as another part of life—children (and adults) will develop more confidence in their own intuition. This in turn is conducive to a more creative and secure personality. A child learns to trust inner hunches about situations and people, building confidence in making and relying on his own decisions.

When the consciousness or awareness of other dimensions expands, practical efficiency expands as well, as there is no division between the spiritual and so-called practical world.

The degree to which your child can successfully link his subconscious "all knowingness" with a conscious day-to-day awareness can be greatly enhanced through your encouraging acceptance.

CHAPTER 2

The Adult/God

Children have more need of models than of critics.

Joubert

THE FIRST INTRODUCTION

You, as a parent, are the introductory reference for your child in learning to relate to the world. Your own self-concept—how you feel about yourself—will have a strong effect on how your child will assess her own confidence, creativity and compassion toward her fellow man. Children are literally mirrors of ourselves! And what a unique and astounding opportunity they offer for our own growth, as well.

From birth to age one and a half your child sees little or no difference between herself and you. Her identity is an extension of yours in the early years.

Your perception of yourself will be reflected to one degree or another in your child. So, if you see yourself as victimized by misfortunes, or if you feel you are not smart enough to do the things you really want to do in life, your child could take on these same thoughts about herself, resulting in an insecure, frustrated and possibly belligerent personality.

All of us feel, at times, as though the world has us defeated and that we simply can't get a grip on things. But if we just take the time, daily, to center ourselves on the fact that we have the potential to do many great and wonderful things, miracles can and will happen—because of our belief in ourselves! This is the secret of true wisdom taught by the ancient Greek philosophers: "Know thyself." They were referring to the vast unlimited capacities we are all rightfully entitled to express.

So, likewise, if you can feel yourself to be a relatively competent and good-hearted individual, and if you practice dwelling on these thoughts often—your child will sense this and will blossom in the radiance of your calm, confident charisma.

You are "god-like" to your child in stature, wisdom and strength. Holistically, your relationship with your child offers you both the greatest opportunity for spiritual growth. If you can be comfortable in this consummate position, living up to your child's godlike expectations can be an inspirational catapult for you. Your child is a channel through which you can be elevated to a new responsible awareness.

THE WORLD'S INPUT

Your child receives many—and often contradictory—models of adulthood from the ever-present and infringing media. Television plays a major part in shaping the child's personality. It is a baby-sitter as well as an information source. Its credibility and its power rival that of the parent.

My toddler once abruptly asked me if the people on the television were inside looking out at her. I realized the impressions adults consider insignificant—the illusion of "people in the television" and "voices in the stereo"—make a powerful impact on children. Sensitive responsibility is required to sort out and explain such stimuli if a child is to grow into a discriminating and fully expressive adult.

One of the beginning steps of truly conscious living for your child and for you would be to monitor your family's television viewing habits. The content of television, for the most part, is poor. But, more importantly, educators agree that it dampens the creative spirit through its ready-made, passive form of entertainment.

One idea would be instead to expose your child to inspirational books on the valiant lives and goals of humanitarians, saints and the noble historical figures; Mother Theresa of Calcutta, Martin Luther King, Jr., Helen Keller, Mahatma Ghandi and Ralph Waldo Emerson are but a few.

Listen to inspirational music of all kinds. Besides classical, there are many "meditation" records and tapes which feature beautiful sitar and flute melodies. Encourage your child to talk about what he feels or imagines while he listens. Also, children love to draw or paint while listening to beautiful music.

SELF-RELIANCE

A strong character cannot be bothered with criticism from others or self-doubt. To cultivate this quality in your child, stress the inportance of standing by her convictions and doing what is right for the benefit of all. Let your child know she can be a shining light in whatever way she choses now, not tomorrow when she's grown, but right now at school or play. Convince her that her life is precious and the world needs her. Help her daily to develop a sense of infinite charisma! She will learn faith in herself and the divine potential of all mankind.

This conviction is not an egotistical delusion, but your child's acceptance of her rightful position as a conscious co-worker in the cosmic scheme of the universe. Man is, generally, unconscious of his role. Thinking that it is "he" versus "the world" magnifies an uneasy feeling of alienation. And this causes him to experience difficulties—lack, limitation, doubt, worry and insecurity. This, then, eventually exhibits in his life as illness, unstable finances, fluctuating emotions and other problems.

On the other hand, by helping your child become aware of the common bond—the Life Force—that unites everyone and everything, you help her develop compassion for humanity as well as strengthening an inner confidence that she is never alone. For when she dares to begin making her own decisions, if she contemplates the ever-present magic of God working through her—she will express herself creatively and freely. How can you go wrong if you affirm only the highest and purest is flowing through you? It is becoming *aware* of it that activates it.

True self-reliance is recognizing there is an eternal support system. But it is also working in cooperation with it as though you had a "Silent Partner" guiding you in your daily affairs.

Train yourself *and* your child to be sensitive to this reality and you will discover the secret of success in any area of your life.

PULLING YOURSELF UP

Naturally, to project a confident image for your child to emulate, what you can begin to do is become extremely aware of your own most casual remarks. Often we become too wrapped up in our own thoughts. We have a mental dialogue going with ourselves concerning errands we have to run, snappy "comebacks" we could have used in a confrontation, anxiety about an upcoming event, and so forth.

When we drift off in our thoughts, our children experience several things. If our thoughts are emotionally charged in a negative way, they feel "hassle vibes" in the atmosphere. Children feel this and sense a lack of harmony, oftentimes becoming irritable and not knowing exactly why.

Also, dwelling too much on our own worries makes us out of touch with what our children are communicating or experiencing. We unconsciously "distance" ourselves from our children. We do this with other adults from time to time, but children are the real victims.

"Well, I can't pay attention to my child every minute! What about me?" you may say. It's true, we can't be totally attentive all the time. But if you are relatively receptive *most* of the time, it will be an investment in the relationship and in your child's character.

Meanwhile, what you do say is being carefully sorted through and absorbed by your watchful little one.

Nothing escapes your child's attention—thoughtless "white lies," under-the-breath slanders and not-so-subtle hypocrisies. He sees, hears and, most importantly, intuitively perceives everything.

Bertrand Russell said, "There should be no enforced respect for grownups. We cannot prevent children from thinking us fools by merely forbidding them to utter their thoughts! In fact, they are more likely to think ill of us if they dare not say so."

Your child has not yet been cluttered or inhibited with the complex workings of the intellect, in the early years. Everything you say is taken quite literally because he sees you as the ideal person. His mind is not sophisticated or "adulterated," so any kidding or even lying about a situation is momentarily believed. In this exchange, the adult is the loser. For the truth of the situation will be discovered sooner or later. And when a child discovers he's been "snowed," his trust in mankind is shaky. If you don't know an answer to his question, admit it.

IT'S HOW WE LIVE, NOT WHAT WE DO

Parents often blame themselves when their children choose different lifestyles or careers or even when their lives look like total disasters.

Do the very best you can for your child in the formative years. Then release her. What happens when she reaches adulthood is her free will choice to create her own life. You can always "be there" as a support, but she needs to make her own decisions as to whether or not she even wants her life to be a success.

One anxiety parents have is, "How do I know if I've done an effective job raising my child?"

The primary goal of the nurturing process is to prepare your young person for mastery of herself and the experiences she encounters.

It really doesn't matter what she chooses to do. What is important is how she masters situations she runs into, no matter what vocation she chooses.

You can effectively raise a child to "fit in" without developing a "milk toast" kid. And your "free thinker" doesn't necessarily have to be a rebel!

So how does your unique and spiritual child fit into a contrary world? "Living in the world, but not of it," an ancient axiom, espouses balancing a *compliant* attitude when dealing with difficult worldly situations with a transcendent *poise and wisdom*, consciously directing life.

Your child's awareness depends on the nurturing she receives in developing her awareness of inter-dimensional reality—that is, her consciousness and her connection with the Infinite.

CHAPTER 3

Brain Factories

All children are born geniuses. It is our educational system that de-geniuses them.

Buckminster Fuller

PUBLIC EDUCATION

It has always been vogue to criticize public institutions, especially the public school systems.

But, the fact is, American public educational systems are teaching a much watered-down version of what's available to be learned. More importantly, we need to examine *how* it's taught.

Reasons for the breakdown in this country's academic institutions are complex. With lower budgets to work within, there are lower salaries, fewer supplies, and crowded classrooms. Lesson plans are safely presented within the limits of publicly accepted, scientifically proven curricula. And education for the masses is naturally going to be slower to accommodate the average intelligence.

The Academically Talented (A.T.) programs are set up to work within the public education system.

Their noteworthy efforts offer creative alternatives for the child whose academic needs require special attention. These programs definitely fulfill a need.

But what's needed is acknowledgment and development of not just those who have special intelligence capacities, but of every child—a new way of crediting each child as having the infinite potential for greatness.

When a child is told, either by parents, siblings or teachers, that he is average, dumb, clumsy, a loser, or a brat, his natural flow of creativity is stopped and he becomes the labels he is called. Likewise, if some children are A.T. students and some are not, the others get the idea that they are "just average."

If we were to treat every child we ever came in contact with as gifted—a divine, intelligent, creative, loving child—what a fantastic generation we would inspire!

Far-sighted educators within the school system and growing numbers of dissatisfied parents are working on this. Clearly, the present system has not been working efficiently. Children are scholastically as well as emotionally immature. Many teens and pre-teens are bored, unmotivated, even suicidal. If a youngster isn't reading or doing simple math by a particular age, he is pushed on through the grades anyway, to face more frustration. Other brighter students who learn quickly and pass their tests easily often become bored if there are no specialized classes for them. For various reasons, the public schools have had a tendency to act as industries, handling children "in bulk"—becoming brain factories, as it were.

EXPAND YOUR CHILD'S
CREATIVE POTENTIAL

"So what am I suppose to do?" you may ask. "I'm not a teacher. Besides, I'm just too busy."

Undoubtedly, American family lifestyles have changed and still are changing radically. Many parents feel the need for a two-income budget. And so with both parents working, an otherwise relaxed home atmosphere is transformed into a "refueling" station for meals and sleeping. Between jobs, school, errands and special school projects, little time is left for parents to assist their children scholastically, emotionally, or spiritually. The teachers feel this unanticipated burden and should not be expected to have to solely address it.

But just as successful finances require careful planning, scheduling 20 minutes or more of your time, several times a week with your young person is a sound investment toward a happy and productive life for your child and you.

You *can* help your child. Teach him to rely on his own intuition. True education is of the spirit! For when the infinite, unlimited aspect of the Self is explored, nothing is a mystery. We are then in touch with self-mastery.

All answers to problems or questions exist within us now. Each of us has access to them now. Amazing, isn't it? We certainly aren't used to thinking this way. But the more we practice relying on our own higher consciousness, the more confident and adept we become.

Many of the great minds who made an impact on

the world were visionary and intuitive. These inventors and reformers utilized (consciously or unconsciously) their intuition. It's been noted they often obtained answers to perplexing problems in a flash of knowing while sleeping or day dreaming.

These answers are like withdrawals from a limitless Universal Consciousness bank. Everyone has an account with this bank, having an infinite number of blank checks available to him. Most people are "missing heirs" to a fantastic inheritance—missing out on all kinds of wondrous things because they just didn't investigate, or were told and believed erroneously, that there is no inheritance.

Your child is naturally creative. As he is allowed and encouraged to realize he already has all the answers, he will find it easier and easier to develop his creativity. Unfortunately, in the early grades and in many pre-schools he is given pre-stenciled pages of figures and told to shade them with particular colors. The message is, "You don't know what to do. This is the way it is supposed to look." When your child is "helped" along in this way, he may become withdrawn and insecure.

Many children are seething little pots of anger. They often feel guilty about their seemingly needless rage. Deep-seated feelings of frustration and destroyed confidence are deadly, stifling all great things they could accomplish. Besides this, suppressed emotional energy, as explained in chapter one, can result in colds, illnesses and other misfortunes.

As you become aware of the need to allow your child *opportunities* to experience his own creativity, you will see how truly rigid our culture's perception of education has been.

DAYDREAMING

Often when children are observed daydreaming or staring blankly, adults and teachers feel compelled to "snap them out of it." This relaxed, effortless state of meditation is vastly out of step with mass consciousness. It triggers vague, uneasy reactions from most adults. Somehow they feel they've lost control.

Actually, these little meditative rest points act as valuable time to reorganize. Your child may be reviewing things that happen to him and the feelings he has about these experiences. He may be using his intuition, picking up someone else's thoughts, or working on a creative idea.

This inward expansion would appear unproductive when compared with the social importance given to outward, visible achievement of goals.

But the purer level of reality requires a child be allowed to engage in the natural meditative state. It is only then that he can joyously merge with the creative and lifegiving flow of pure consciousness. He is then beyond reach of the stress of worry, guilt and fear.

When children are conditioned to rely solely on external sources for information, neglecting their own inner latent wisdom, they develop insecurities and neuroses. This is evident in the growing number of worldly two- and three-year-olds who know television commercials verbatim and *believe* the messages they deliver. They get caught in a treadmill of false values and bogus anxieties; to be "sleek and sexy" and to beware, "this is the flu season."

HOLISTIC EDUCATION

Experimental or "open door" schools are really nothing new. There has always been a certain percentage of parents who prefer to have their children taught privately either because of necessity (living in a rural environment) or choice (conviction they can do a better job).

In Phoenix, Arizona the "Wide Horizons Educational Center," directed by Carol Clark-Keppler, describes its approach as "holistic." They propose, "Our emphasis is not on teaching facts but on teaching students to *think* so they can see meaning in facts . . . We encourage creativity—a sensitivity to problems, fluency of ideas and originality of interpretation. This is a gifted program designed for all."

In Tempe, Arizona the "Awakening Seed" offers an "academy for young children . . . dedicated to the idea that children learn best in an environment which allows them to express themselves creatively within a carefully planned program."

The blueprint for our approach to life itself is drawn up in our early years with our parents and the schools. If early learning is superficial—that is, certain subjects are taught yet some are avoided (topics considered too controversial or too spiritual to address) we miss a whole exciting dimension of learning. If subjects are separated and segregated, totally ignoring the silver thread of Life, which unites everything that exists, how can we ever expect our lives to flow harmoniously?

We are so much more than our physical bodies. Our very existence is multi-demensional—proven through Kirilan photography and other scientific discoveries in the field of parapsychology. Yet many of us are afraid to admit we are spiritual, that we all have a common bond, making us *non*-sectarian.

Because of this refusal to admit our One-ness, the intolerance of one group's beliefs towards another's has created an educational paralysis. No one wants to step on anyone else's dogma! It's as if we tip-toe around any reference to our Creator, the Common Bond which unites all living creatures. The result is a fact-filled, dry curriculum that often fails to challenge the student's higher learning potentials.

We are expressions of Universal Consciousness, by the very nature of our "Being." It would therefore seem only natural to introduce young people to the world with a feeling of Cosmic Unity. Science, mathematics, linguistics, the arts and spiritual truth are but different rays of the same Light Source.

Guide your child to fully express her finer sensitities. As she applies her inherently divine sense of wisdom and understanding in approaching practical, daily experiences—she will know no limits!

CHAPTER 4

Relating

INSECURITY

One of the more difficult steps of growth for any-one—child or adult—is dealing with insecurity. The natural trendency to compare ourselves with others is the most insidious, self-defeating habit we can allow ourselves to be caught up in. Perhaps you re-member a childhood friend who always had so many friends and you wondered why you didn't. Maybe you've experienced professional jealousy as an adult, or perhaps you've brooded over going to a social situation where you feel you don't quite fit in. We've all experienced self-doubt to some degree.

Be watchful that this is not allowed to get a foot-hold in your child's consciousness. Help him build an unshakable foundation based on the fact that he is the co-creator of his world. No matter where he goes he will be totally confident—because he is One with all. Remind him several times a day that his Heavenly Father will always assist him. His invisi-ble Ally is always at his side.

Affirm to him he can *accomplish anything* with this Secret Power supporting him. If you communi-cate this Truth with enthusiasm, truly wonderful things will unfold; for belief is the doorway to miracles.

Support, don't criticize, your child's decisions. If you have one of those unique children who knows, unshakably, what he wants to do with his life—support him, despite any feelings you may have that he has a greater or different destiny. Or, if your inquisitive child jumps from one interest to another it could be he is learning more than if he were to stay with just one project!

Remember that your child can sense your feelings and thoughts. So, when his interests or goals don't turn out as well as he expected, watch your reactions and responses. Be mindful not to project the feeling that he's failed, for there really is no such thing as failure. Help him to see the value in all experiences. Our most difficult experiences, our most unpleasant relationships offer the greatest opportunities for growth. Children may experience disappointments, but they don't have a sense of failure until they learn it from adult reactions. It is a social, learned response that can and should be transcended.

A young man wanted to become editor of his school newspaper. His capable dedication and ambition intimidated his staff. Eventually, he found himself working on the paper alone. Hours and hours of pasting up and solitary writing led to feelings of resentment and frustration. After a time he realized he couldn't continue to work with this arrangement and he reluctantly resigned.

An unthinking parent could have made the remark, ''Why do you let people use you? They don't care.'' The implication is, ''You are spineless. You've been made a fool of.''

A more constructive approach would be to ask, ''What did you learn from this experience?'' Or the parent could build the young person's confidence by saying, "I admire your high ideals, your ambition and your willingness to shoulder the responsibility for such a project. Maybe there was a lesson for you to learn about leadership. Delegating responsibility to others is an ability you might want to learn more about."

A sensitive parent might also want to point out that a truly successful project is launched and sustained through the dedication of all participants. Learning to appraise the priorities of others in relation to your own is an art in itself.

Children as well as adolescents often go through the game of being ostracized from the "in-crowd" or even from a favorite friend who, for no apparent reason, turns "cold."

Counseling your child to try to force or "bribe" her way into a group with candy or a party, or urging her to find new friends, will confirm her fears that it is necessary to be accepted by those "out there." This puts a misplaced value on the importance of social link-ups. Her worth as a divine Being is undermined by attributing undue importance to social success—popularity, conforming with friends' expectations, living in the "right" neighborhood, and so forth.

In allowing others to determine our acceptability, we will always come up short in one way or another. So this is why it is important to teach your child that she is special and perfect *exactly* as she is, while inspiring her toward *her* highest goals.

Several times my youngest daughter was coaxed by my oldest daughter to join her, coloring in the coloring books. She continually showed reluctance and I began to wonder what was wrong. It turned out that someone at a preschool—a child, a teacher, or a teacher's aide—had stressed to her not to "scribble." She was developing tremendous anxiety not only about scribbling, but also about which color was the *proper* color to use in a drawing. She was developing a type of creative paralysis at the age of three. At age five there should be some discipline expected, but not at this age.

Not only is it important to scribble in the early stages of motor skills, but it is equally essential for a child's feelings of confidence to be unshakably established!

After working with her on a few deliberate anything-goes scribbling sessions, she began to feel free again. Now she is quite creative with her art work.

Aside from teaching your child how special she is, stress that *everyone* is precious as well. Spiritual egotism—thinking we are more special than someone else—can be just as damaging as emotional insecurity. So when your child has difficulties relating to peer pressure, teach her patience. Tell her, "Other children are learning, too. You can be their 'quiet teacher' through your example and by gently encouraging them to do what is best for their growth—whatever is harmonious and positive." Remind your child that she should always be ready to learn from others as well!

RESPONSIBILITY

Stockpiling material possessisons can easily become a preoccupation with your child. It can dominate her thoughts, her drives, her very life as she grows into adulthood. Happiness itself becomes dependent on whether or not that new toy or pair of jeans is acquired. And often, when that desired object is obtained, an unexplainable depression settles in. That great satisfaction that was expected to come with possessing this item is not experienced!

Most people work hard all their lives to achieve a solid, secure career, a nice home and some kind of retirement plan. And this is all they're concerned with. Some achieve this. Many others feel they have to struggle just to survive. But, inevitably, everyone—the wealthy and the improverished alike —faces the same common moment of self-confrontation. "Now what?" we ask. "There must be more than this!"

Days spent in selfish indulgence result in misery. Without commitment and without concern for our connection with *all*, life can become a hell on earth. When the emphasis is placed solely on acquisition, the experience soon becomes stagnant. The secret of vitality and joy in living is not found through getting things, but in savoring the immortal beauty and love that permeates all living things.

In many schools now there is a growing awareness among educators that young people are over-exposed to materialism, irresponsibility and an irreverance for life.

At O. K. Adcock Elementary School in Las Vegas, Nevada, principal Richard Masek is one of those educators who, "teach(es children) kindness to animals along with reading, writing and arithmetic... For example, mathematical calculations on the number of possible offspring non-sterilized animals produce offers a multiplication exercise.

" 'This is supplemental education—character training—that teaches the value of kindness and reverence for all forms of life,' Masek said.

"Masek pointed out that in our society animals

(pets) are thought of as consumer items and the result of this attitude is a huge waste of life that costs taxpayers many millions of dollars each year.

" 'Pet stores proliferate in our society and so do euthanasia rooms,' Masek said. . . . 'Pets are routinely bought and dumped when no longer wanted.' "

Sensitive teaching such as this is exemplary of how your young person's awareness of his own personal responsibility can be heightened—towards pets, belongings and himself.

Siri Satya Sai Baba, the Indian avatar, states, "The father and mother must supplement at home the training given by teachers at school. . . They (children) must also be trained to have a sense of responsibility for their personal belongings.".

Sai Baba's spiritual approach to education is drastically changing the face and the future of India. Children graduate from those schools not only with outstanding academic marks, but also with radiant spiritual maturity.

Responsibility for things around us is not a possessive responsibility. We are taking care of business for the Creator as a competent babysitter would. None of our possessions are really ours. Yet we have the highest duty to care for all life as expressions of the Source.

WE ARE SOUL

Teach your child the transitory nature of *all* things. Inspire him to be great, rather than putting so much attention on having great things, no matter what the cost. It's fine to have possessions but remind him that all externals in this dimension, this day-to-day world, are in a continual processs of change. Every single thing he has he will tire of, eventually. Toys break, clothes wear out, friends move away. Even you, a seemingly permanent fixture in this world, change from moment to moment.

So what does he have? The only things that really endure are his inner experiences. And it is these investments of time and energy toward self-realization that help him unfold his true nature as eternal soul. This is true security!

Once the light dawns that we are not a body housing a soul (in some vague area of the head or chest), but rather we are Soul clothed in a body—we are then truly free to view ourselves and the universe objectively.

Soul (some call it the superconscious mind) is not an organ or a gland. It is the invisible power of our collective wisdom, our creativity, our compassion for and connection with all life.

We are soul—that invisible intelligence, gathering experiences in a continuous state of growth. The body is used by soul for the purpose of expanding consciousness.

There are no boundaries, no limitations, and no point where you leave off and another being begins. We are all One and yet retain individual awareness. This may be difficult to understand at first. It can be more easily grasped if you try to *feel* what it means.

So, as you are One with everything, it becomes meaningless (actually, ridiculous) to strive to acquire things when you are *already* One with all! Everything is available to you in Divine Order, much as a library lends itself available for your growth. It is the straining and struggling to acquire that which is *already* ours that causes so much un-necessary misery.

LONELINESS

Teach your child how to deal with loneliness in this way also. As he is One with all of life, there is no separation from anyone or anything. There are only the apparent changes of this dimension. Every-one around us—even those people we have difficulty with—are playing different roles within the same Cosmic Family . As relationships change—friends drop away, new acquaintances are introduced—help your child realize that this life is like a movie; that we are all actors with various roles to play. And in playing these roles, we learn about tolerance, under-standing and compassion. We all have a very real re-lationship "off camera." This "connection" is the God-Self within each of us. By practicing this aware-ness, your child will become so unshakable in his confidence and inner serenity nothing will trip him up.

We don't really need anything or anyone outside of ourselves for our survival or well being. But there is a certain fellowship, a universal love that we ex-tend to assist our peers in reaching their highest po-tential simply because we are connected with one another in divine expression. To help and love one another is to expand one's own radiance to infinity.

Your child should be made aware of his direct re-sponsibility in disciplining his own actions. Teach the cosmic law of cause and effect, the Golden Rule —as a law of physics. It is an exacting law of the uni-verse. Do unto others as you would have them do unto you. For every action there is an equal and opposite reaction. There is no separation between the laws of physics and spiritual truth.

These truths can be taught in informal situations, such as riding in the car, while having meals or getting dressed. Talk casually about the importance of showing kindness to others as well as how unkind words and acts have a way of ''boomerang-ing'' on the sender.

GUILT

A clear understanding of the law of cause and effect, that it is an impersonal law responding to any thought, word or act, will enable children to learn valuable lessons without guilt.

Many of us were raised with notions of retribution, suffering for one's sins, and, in Eastern thought, paying off a karmic burden. Punishment-consciousness generates mass guilt and fear. Those who have been entrenched with this defeatist misery have convinced themselves they will never be worthy to experience love, happiness, prosperity, success and spiritual wisdom. Those who feel they don't deserve it will often subconsciously as well as directly, sabotage themselves when they get too close to their heart's desire! It's often considered normal to have difficulties and odd to have an orderly, harmonious life.

Everyone has the capacity for greatness—to experience their fondest dreams, to have perfect health and stimulating relationships. Once we believe this—with enthusiasm—this is what the experience will be! As the great American philosopher Ralph

Waldo Emerson said, "Man is what he thinks all day."

Guilt and fear are the most mentally destructive and physically depleting emotions there are. Emmet Fox, author and lecturer, once said, "The forgiveness of sins is the central problem of life. Sin is a separation from God, and it is the tragedy of human experience. It is a sense of isolated, self-regarding, personal existence, whereas the Truth of Being is that all is One."

If your child is feeling unworthy or lacking confidence because of some past event, remind him that the present moment is really all there is. The past is a recording of an experience in the mind. By dwelling on an unfortunate event, that event is magnified, because that is where the attention is. So, in looking backward, bemoaning a past situation or relationship, the joy of the present is missed. If there was a pertinent lesson in that past incident to learn from, guide your child to scan the experience objectively as he would a how-to book and apply it to his situation now. This should be the only reason for looking back.

Explain to your child that when he's overly critical with himself he's not relating to the Truth of his Being, which is a manifestation of God! Help him to be kind to himself, knowing all the while he can be working on those areas of his personality that need it.

PEER PRESSURE

Of course, there will always be stumbling blocks in growing up—acne, homework, boyfriend/girlfriend problems, and so forth. Assist him in developing a detached perspective, an objective attitude, and never let him forget his true identity—the immortal Self—and that all things can be overcome.

Total awareness entails being watchful of every thought, word and action of every day. We live in a physical dimension, where the laws of cause and effect are operative. Yet our higher nature is beyond this—stronger than any negative situation that can come up. The trick is to play the game effectively, keeping in mind that it is, indeed, a game. This is the right application of the Buddhist approach to living the "middle path," balance in all things.

Teach your child to generate kindness, tolerance, freedom, wisdom and happiness. But also teach him that his negative emotions will create negative experiences for him. Not as punishment, but as a direct result of his frame of mind. This is what's referred to as the "mirror effect," explained more fully in chapter five.

Many parents worry about children's susceptibility to sexual explicitness in the media. There are several things to keep in mind when dealing with this situation. The first is to instill in your child—the earlier the better—a strong sense of personal pride, honor and self-respect. This is achieved through building a positive self-image through praise, encouragement and love from you. Secondly, you must trust that the strength of his own moral fiber will carry him through any experience. If you have no trust in him, he will feel it. Relax and know he is guided; because fear will give energy to a situation that will dissolve on its own. Thirdly, take active responsibility in monitoring what's being "fed" into their "computers" while they're young.

Many advertisements and commercials motivate the viewer to be "sexy." You might explain to your young person that this is just to sell their product, adding, "Remember, you are more than just a body. Being sexy or pretty is not the most important thing in the world. Being graceful, noble and helping those who need help is the highest aspiration you can strive for.

"Your body is special. Everything you do, every day, should be directed to keep it strong and healthy. Make certain everything you do is accompanied with thoughts of love and harmony."

Children are especially vulnerable to the unkind feedback of other children. Point out to your child that her friends may try to pressure her to do certain things just so she can be their friend. The tension can get rough. But she will have to live with herself long after her friends are gone.

THE INVISIBLE ALLIANCE

Remind her that she is never alone. She has a special, secret Friend, who if called upon, will give her the strength and the joyous attitude that will help her fly over any difficulty as an eagle glides gracefully over canyon walls.

Tell her she is wonderful! She is a valuable instrument for the upliftment of mankind. Day by day, this builds a powerful strength in her psyche that can be felt by those around her. She becomes an inspiration!

As William Shakespeare wrote: "To thine own self be true, and it must follow, as the night the day, thou canst not then be false to any man."

CHAPTER 5

The Mirror of Life

THE HEART'S DESIRE

There is nothing more exciting or challenging in the world than to know your life is totally in your hands, to realize your life can be full of exciting adventures and wonderful opportunities. Your highest goals, all those things you secretly want to accomplish, are all available to you now, not later when you have more education, when you're older, or for any other reason. As with a blank video-tape in a brand new camera, you have the power to create any program imaginable.

So why settle for less? Why settle for being average or even somewhat successful instead of being a TOTAL success in every way? Somewhere along the line, an authority figure—a relative or a teacher— gave you the idea you probably wouldn't realize your wildest dreams. According to the law of averages you would probably lead an average life like everyone else, fraught with problems and difficulties. And, perhaps being vulnerable at that point, you accepted this as the way things are. And as we believe, so it comes to pass.

The lesson here is that when we agree—even momentarily—with someone else's assessment of what they think is true we give *their* idea power, or energy. And—presto! It manifests—you incorporate this attitude in your life, according to your belief in what other people tell you.

For example, Sue generally had harmonious dealings with strangers in her daily excursions of running errands. Sue was also somewhat vulnerable to what her close friend, Annie, would tell her. So, when Annie told her, ''You know, Sue, times are getting tough and people aren't as nice as they used to be. Everybody's for their own skin! And you, being so sweet and kind, are an easy target for manipulative people!'' Sue, taking in every word of her ''friend's'' now has two new ideas. First, she's an easy target. And second, more and more people are out to get you. Now, she runs her errands with anxiety, making certain to keep a cool distance in all her dealings. Those with whom she deals feel this and respond with reservation. So now we have two parties in a standoff.

If we anticipate rejection, abuse or arguments—even subconsciously—we will get it!

You have the power to change experiences in your life through *consciously* developing strong, unwavering faith in yourself and your fellow man. You will always be protected through complete reliance on the guidance of Infinite Intelligence, which is available to everyone. In so doing, you will experience harmonious and efficient transactions daily.

YOUR CHILD'S SELF-IMAGE

There is a beautifully simple way to explain to your child the power of his own self image.

As you see yourself, so the world reponds to you.
This is what is referred to in metaphysics as the
"mirror effect." If your child sees himself as loving,
good, kind, successful and prosperous—invisible vibrations, thought forms are transmitted from him.
It can be heard in his voice, seen in his eyes, felt in
his presence. People around him feel this—consciously and/or unconsciously—and reflect back to
him what he is putting out, as a mirror would.

You, as a parent or educator, can be a conscious
co-programmer with your child. Help him initiate a
creative, intelligent, positive self-image. Your
words have incredible power and shape your child's
self-confidence for life. This isn't meant to scare
you, but to inspire you on to the most responsible
challenge you may ever encounter to help your
child be all that he can be.

Tell your child several times daily that he is gifted.
He is creative. He is kind and he is beautiful. Tell
him you know he can do great things and that he
has a successful life ahead of him!

The mirror effect could also be called the "magnet
effect." If you find yourself in a confused state—
that is, you've allowed yourself to become confused—you will draw to you confused thought forms
of other people, as a magnet attracts metal filings.

SECURE THOUGHTS = HAPPY ENVIRONMENT

Cultivate a clear thinking mind and the world
around you will be well-ordered.

When a child hears, "Don't go over there. You'll
fall!" or "Put on your coat, or you'll catch a cold!",

depending on how susceptible to suggestion the child is at that moment, his behavior will be a self-fulfilling prophecy. He also receives a fearful vibration of insecurity from the adult saying these things.

Fear is an extremely powerful creative force. Thoughts alone do manifest. But thoughts coupled with emotion—fear, excitement, enthusiasm, joy —create much faster! Your child's acceptance of a powerfully projected thought will create that thought in his life.

Ideas are energy. Ideas are the creative force for all things visible. Science declares the entire universe— planets, stars, galaxies, novas, gaseous clouds, even black holes—is made up of varying degrees of energy. You as a miniature universe—organs, muscles, tissue, blood, emotions, experiences—are bound together with vibrations of energy, too. Control your energy—that is, your thoughts and emotions—and you control your universe.

Scientific laboratory studies have shown that emotional attitudes affect hormone secretions of the pineal gland, located near the center of the brain. The pineal gland has been referred to as the master gland because it stimulates all the other glands and therefore the overall health of the body.

The effect of the emotions and mental attitude on the aura (electromagnetic field) can be measured in terms of physical strength by means of psycho-kinesis (p.k.) testing. It has been found, as yogis have taught throughout the ages, when one feels insecure or lacking in confidence, the aura (depicted in religious art as the halo) weakens or shrinks. Well-disciplined individuals have long known that strength is not a matter of muscles. True strength comes with inner poise and stamina. It is with these two valiant traits that your child will vanquish any obstacle or crisis.

This simple exercise can help you explain to your child how the world responds exactly to what he projects. Ask him to stand before a mirror and close his eyes for a moment. Tell him to think about something that makes him very angry. Now ask him to open his eyes and look at himself. He may laugh after seeing his irate expression. If only we could laugh at ourselves when getting angry in real life situations!

But, just as the mirror, the world doesn't know you're kidding. It reflects back exactly what it receives. It "gets angry back."

A little puppy will bark angrily at his own reflection in a pool of water until he realizes it's just a small part of reality. He then leaves with a mature realization.

It should be stressed that there is nothing wrong with getting furious with situations or individuals who push our patience to the limit. But, teach your child not to waste his energy on excessive anger, depression or worry over trivial things. Then he's no different than a silly little dog barking into a pond.

You are striving to build in your child's consciousness an awareness of life beyond the mirror, beyond the surface of the water's reflection.

Our three-dimensional world can be compared to a one-way glass. It appears to be reflective, like a mirror, yet there is another dimension on the other side. The little puppy could only see what was reflected back to him, never daring to wonder or see carefully the depth (the other dimension) of the water. There was a whole other world beyond his own reflection!—a world of different life forms, experiences, a whole different point of view than he was used to. But he was too involved in his own world, his own reactions, to expand his awareness into another world.

Therefore, to get in touch with this level of awareness, we must relax (stop the barking). Let go of anxiety and *effortlessly* allow the vision to expand. The more we wonder what is beyond this physical dimension, the more it will become evident to us.

DEATH

To those who have died, or have gone to the other side of the one-way glass, we might very well look like silly little puppies. They watch us going about our lives, worrying over what we'll eat, what we'll wear, whether we made enough money to pay the bills—barking, barking, barking, not realizing there's a whole other world where these concerns don't matter.

Those living on the other side, watching us, are aware of their world *and* ours. They often try to knock on the glass to get our attention, to wake us up to the reality of another world. But unless we relax and allow our awareness, our consciousness to expand, to reach out with heightened senses, we won't be able to hear their knocking. We won't wake up to the fact there are, indeed, other worlds, just as real as this and that we can be learning from their beneficial vantage point—if we but listen. They are all around us, separated by frequency only.

There is no death, *per se*. This is only a limited understanding of the transitions most make from dimension to dimension. It can be compared to dreaming—going to sleep in one world and awakening in another. The cosmic cycle continues in this way, offering more and more adventure to the awakening dreamer, until he becomes so adept, he need not go to sleep anymore, but merely transports the physical body wherever he wishes by altering the vibratory level.

As a child, my first encounter with death—that of a great-grandfather—impressed me with the needlessness of it. "Why die?" I wondered. And I know most children wonder and struggle with this inevitable event.

I felt the Master Jesus' message through his magnificent Resurrection was widely misunderstood. He continually inspired his disciples and anyone who listens with the timeless challenge, "He that believeth on me, the works that I do shall he do also; and greater works than these shall he do . . ." (John 14:12).

The body is really energy—molecules, rotating around each other at a relatively slow rate of speed. So, the body looks solid, although it is not. Therefore it is infinitely changeable. If it were not, there would never be healings (see chapter six). The body is changeable, healable and immortal by nature. It becomes inflexible, sick and dies due to our own acceptance of negative thoughts, lack of preventive maintenance, and belief in death, sickness and misery.

Physical immortality is the ultimate challenge of mankind. "The last enemy to overcome is death" was a personal message to you and me. There are many "immortals." Besides Jesus, there is Babaji, of the White Brotherhood, now in India, several in what was Tibet, some of the mystics mentioned in the Mormon literature, and many more less prominent. And there will be many more.

I would strongly discourage anyone telling their child he must die. The body is capable of infinite regeneration. And although this is not a widely accepted concept—you might tell your child to keep it under his hat to avoid common ridicule—it nevertheless is a valid and practiced art.

Tell your child he will always "be." No matter what happens—earthquakes, war, famine—he will always exist, in one dimension or another. He will never cease to learn, experience and grow. He will always be discovering more and more of his true, immortal nature. Once he realizes this eternal Truth he will experience an unshakable feeling of confidence and courage.

"For Life and Death are one, even as the river and sea are one."   Kahlil Gibran.

CHAPTER 6

Healing

All healings—medical, nutritional, psychic, spiritual—are valuable. Good health should be maintained and sometimes it takes a combination of methods to sustain it. Ideally, we want our children and ourselves to achieve total mastery over bodily health. But, we need not be condescending toward the medical profession. If we do need medical attention from time to time, be thankful that the Creative Intelligence works through many different channels making our healings available.

To understand the process of self-healing we need to know more about health itself and exactly what happens when we've allowed ourselves to become sick.

Health is not a rare commodity to be achieved or worked toward. Perfect health is a natural state to be *allowed to express*. The body is a natural self-healing organism that channels healing energy and life-giving hormones throughout the body.

As we sleep, the conscious mind is put aside. Yet all the functions of the body are taken care of. Although we are not aware of it, we continue to breathe, the heart pumps, and the entire body rejuvenates itself. So the natural tendency is self-healing without any conscious effort on our part.

Children are natural healers. When sick, they recover quickly. Their broken bones mend sooner. And they are amazingly resilient during crises. True, they are growing and the quick healing processes can be linked in part to that fact.

But they are also more in tune with the subconscious. They haven't as yet picked up the abundance of mental poisons most adults entertain. An illustration of this is when Jesus said, "Suffer the little children to come unto me, and forbid them not; for such is the kingdom of heaven." (Mark 10:14) Children are the example of "the kingdom." They are models of faith, innocence, trust and joy. All of these are traits of one who maintains perfect health in Divine Order.

Perfect health is natural. Sickness is unnatural and inharmonious. It seems ridiculous to have to point this out, yet on a subconscious level many are even afraid of being 100 per cent healthy. It's as if one is expected to have a certain number of colds a year. Most people like to have a "buffet of discomforts" they can rattle off to their friends, as if there were nothing else to discuss. And others like to have just one or two "safe" complaints so they won't be left out of the social exchange.

WHY WE GET SICK

When our thoughts, feelings and irresponsible actions introduce negativity—anger, resentment, insecurity, as well as health abuses such as overindulgence in alcohol, drugs, smoking, etc.—to the body, we interfere with the healing process. Disease is really being at dis-ease with ourselves and the world. Tension and anxiety render us more vulnerable to ideas of illness, which then manifest in us.

All thoughts result in manifestation—especially if the ideas are held for a period of time with *emotion*.

Germs and viruses have an undeniable reality. Their spores can be studied in laboratories under microscopes. They have actual dimension. But where did they come from? Their origin is due to collective fear thoughts by large groups of people generating energy (attention, usually fear) toward illness or disease. Telethons and fund drives feed interest in disease as do all the myriad remedies in the markets.

Therefore, if we hold the idea of being subject to illness or disease and hold that thought with fear or anxiety, it will come to pass in our experience—that is, unless we take firm, conscious control of our own thinking processes! If we think ourselves vulnerable, we will be vulnerable. "The thing which I greatly feared has come upon me," was the lament of Job in the Bible. And it's a timeless grievance.

Thus, if you or your child see others getting colds or various types of flu and you acknowledge this, it gains power in the family's consciousness. From what you believe, your child will pick up a certain percentage through mental osmosis. The experience will then be magnified in your family.

Just because certain diseases and illnesses have a certain popularity with the masses doesn't mean you and your child are necessarily subject to them. You *can* be the exception in your group through understanding basic metaphysics—that all form originates in thought; and that by being aware and in control of what you are thinking and feeling you shape your own destiny. This is the secret of mastery. Self-healing is often the first demonstration by many who have gone on to higher expressions of divine radiance. The choice is yours, now!

Teach your child to understand the significance of his thoughts, which are more real than the ground beneath him.

The art of pure, positive thinking is rarely taught our children. One positive idea or feeling can shatter any aspect of negativity like a laser beam explodes a clay jar.

Self-healings take place much faster if the subject is honest with him/herself. It's important to determine if a healing is really wanted. Perhaps the subject thinks he wants a healing when he is actually enjoying the attention, sympathy, etc. gained from having an ailment. Secondly, can the subject sincerely unravel the origins of the negative traits that caused the affliction, and is he willing to use the positive affirmations or thoughts to reverse the manifestation? For what is created can be dissolved.

All illness or disease has basic roots in low self-image. Below is a chart of negative feelings, their effects and suggested thoughts to hold for healing.

When any of these symptoms are displayed in children, it is because of the thought forms in the present environment—tense, anxious mental images of those around him—and/or ancestral attitudes. For example, the thought forms of a relative, who held a cynical, bitter view of his fellow man, can be passed down genetically through mental osmosis, showing up as diabetes in a small child. (Remember it is a medical fact that emotional/

NEGATIVE FEELING	EFFECT	SUGGESTED HEALING TREATMENT
Rejection, confusion frustration, anger, feeling misunderstood	Colds, pneumonia, eye, nose & throat problems, asthma, T.B.	Say, "I love everyone and I cannot be hurt." "His truth shall be my shield and buckler."
Painful memories, not wanting to accept a situation	Diarrhea	Everything that has happened is O.K. Accept the past. Live in the *now*.
Stubborness, limitation, mental tension, holding onto a situation or person	Constipation	Practice living lightly and joyfully. Study and practice tolerance.
Insecurity, lack of confidence, no support from others	Problems with feet and legs	Say, "Listen . . . Be still and know I am God" and "If God be for me, who can be against me?"
Irritating circumstances & relationships, resentment, bitterness, hatred	Skin eruptions, acne allergies, heart trouble, stiff joints	"My skin is an envelope for Infinite Life; I radiate health." "To err is human, to forgive is divine."

Impatience, nervousness, excessive sensitivity, greed, excessive materialism	Poor hearing, poor vision, migraines, high blood pressure, heart attacks	Say, "I rejoice in the Light and Sounds of Creation. All things are clear to me. I see and hear Truth." Inhale and Exhale, "Peace."
Cynicism, pessimism, defeatism, lack of love expression in the environment	Diabetes, kidney disorders, polio, anemia, low blood pressure	Cultivate joy in living. Meditate on love. Say, "Father I love you."
Fear, guilt, depression	"Accidents," cancer, personal failure, poverty	Say, "I give thanks that I am divinely guided & prospered in all my ways."
Inferiority, introversion, antagonism	Lack of friends, "accidents," allergies, headaches	Say, "I am a Center of radiant divine light."
Anxiety over money, children, the future	Insomnia, ulcers, colitis	Feel a powerful, loving river of peace flowing through you, bringing love, truth and beauty. Say, "I rest in peace, wake in joy, and live in God."

mental conditions have healing as well as degenerative influence on glandular secretions.) Genetics is more than a physical condition passed along family lines. Deeply entrenched beliefs and attitudes passed on from generation to generation manifest as either illnesses, diseases or a carefree, happy personality.

POSITIVE TREATMENT

Many so-called terminal illnesses and incurable diseases have been and are being dissolved daily. Individuals ridden with cancer and given a few months to live have rejected the prognosis, thrown everything they have into the power of their own faith and have experienced miraculous recoveries!

In actuality, healing is simple. Our belief that it is difficult makes it so. At the core of effective healing is the attitude one must adopt—that is to become as little children once again. Learn to trust implicitly that everything is in perfect and divine order.

When we agree with or accept uncontrolled thoughts of mass consciousness, our health is in jeopardy. But what we create we can uncreate with cleansing, purifying thoughts of ourselves as divine expression of the Creator!

Of course, this requires self-discipline, a keen sense of inner awareness of what you believe and what you're experiencing. Most of us have been so mesmerized from childhood to believe in sickness, that we need to analyze, confront and extricate these habitual attitudes. They've been snowballing for centuries.

It takes incredible courage to build and maintain

faith in an invisible Power when all the evidence around us is contradictory. This is why when Jesus healed the blind man he told him to go his way and tell no one, because doubtful reactions could neutralize the healing.

Keep your child from putting his attention on diseases or illness. Tell him often the healing presence of God is always with him.

Here is a simple health maintenance exercise for your child to practice. Have him sit down and close his eyes and visualize healing energy pouring in through the top of the head clear down the spinal column as he inhales deeply. Then, on the exhale, have him imagine the light pouring out through the forehead as a powerful beam. Continue inhaling and exhaling at least ten times. In order to guide the exercise, you might want to ring a small bell for each breath cycle so he is not distracted by trying to keep track of how many breaths he's taken.

Talk with your child about how the body is the divine vehicle used to experience life in this dimension. Maintain it as you would any other useful tool you'd need for a job. You don't put pancake syrup in your gas tank or pour shampoo in your mouth when you're hungry. So, too, avoid dumping negative thoughts into the mind. They only weaken and destroy nerves and glands, making the body vulnerable to illness. A car is easier to replace than a body. How negligent we are sometimes in maintaining the most important vehicle we operate in this plane of existence!

As our thinking becomes clarified—as we become more harmonious with positive energy currents, we will be exposed to and attracted to healthier diets.

Processed junk food will hold less and less appeal. It's a natural law: where the attention is, everything else will follow.

Keeping a constant vigilance on our thoughts takes practice at first until it "locks in" and becomes more automatic, as any habit would with persistence. If children start early, demonstrating control over the physical body through objectively checking the emotions they, indeed, will get a head start on self-mastery.

CHAPTER 7

Adaptability

Species survival in any world—the sea kingdom, plant life, the evolution of man—depends on how that organism adapts to its environment. If a life form can flow with life's demands in an easy, effortless, efficient manner its endurance is guaranteed.

DISCIPLINE THROUGH LOVE

In order for your child to more readily adapt to society, discipline is essential.

It can be quite unnerving when a thirty- or forty-pound child emotionally upsets an adult through temper tantrums, balkiness and continuous demands for attention; but these heated displays of a child's increasing independence are indeed necessary.

Children have a natural survival instinct to express themselves. And often adults are so engrossed in their own routines and schedules that they forget all people have this need—even children. If children feel they are not being considered in daily routines they will rebel! It's no accident these rebellions take place when you are in a hurry or in public.

Adults go on strike or walk out when they feel

their employer is not considerate of their condition or viewpoint. Countless marriages break up for the same reason.

It's a tricky situation. Somehow, in the emotionalism of a confrontation, try to have compassion for what your child is feeling. But also establish clear rules for behavior with others—that is, respect for *you* as well as society at large.

Generations weaned on the liberal "Spockism" of the 1950's came into young adulthood craving discipline and guidelines. Some turned to drugs for escape, others to religious cults that gave them instant ritualistic familial roots.

Even now, as the New Age dawns, there are surprisingly numerous so-called awakened ones who raise children with so much unbalanced awe of them as "souls" that there is little discipline or guidance in social graces and respectful etiquette! After all, they feel, these are "high souls" who may be teaching them—the parents. As a result, many such children grow into rude, self-centered, unhappy young people.

At the other end of the spectrum, there are those who feel children are little more than "wild animals," as an acquaintance of mine so sensitively put it. Extremists of this philosophy contend that little ones must conform to an adult-oriented world at the cost of beatings. These are the adults with their egos on the line, who are anxious that they must maintain 100 percent control at all costs, lest the child make a fool of them.

An interesting footnote to this is that many adults often disguise jealousy of their child—wishing they were carefree and unencumbered by social rules—

through over-disciplining when the child isn't doing anything terribly wrong. Sensitive discrimination requires the adult to determine if the child is merely expressing herself or if she is deliberately being disruptive.

The following is a check-list of disciplinary principles to help you get a clear, balanced relationship with your child—a relationship emphasizing mutual respect and a cooperative spirit.

1. Before disciplining, first get clear within yourself what kind of behavior you expect. (Do you move all your breakables away for the first five years—or do you leave them out and expect your child not to touch? This is a personal decision, of course. Some parents would rather avoid as much confrontation as possible, doing without home adornment for a few years. Others would rather not make that sacrifice. You decide.)

2. *Why* are you disciplining? Are you flying off the handle because of a stress situation that's eating at you? Then your disciplining techniques will be inconsistent. Your child could turn into a confused and angry teenager.

3. Be firm, not harsh, in what you expect. There is a difference! Follow through on punishment procedures.

4. Clearly communicate, at a neutral time, what you expect from your child. *Before* going into a public place, explain how you want your child to behave. For example don't use vague, abstract terms such as "Be good." Get her eye contact and say, "I

want you to stay in your seat, keep your voice low, color with your pencils or look at a book. I know you'll act nicely so we can go out more often."

5. Don't take children into adult-oriented situations for extended periods of time and expect them to keep still. How would you like to be forced into a boring situation? A small child sitting with a group of adults should have something to occupy herself. But she should not be expected to be seen and not heard for a two-hour gab session.

6. Feed your child continuous praise regarding her self-worth, her intelligence, her kindness to others. Tell her how you love it when she listens to you, and how you know she'll always be guided and protected. The more energy you pour into this phase of disciplining, the less punishment you'll have to administer.

7. Although there should be no need for physical violence in punishing a child, once in a while a child will push and push above and beyond passive disciplinary measures. "Time out" alone in a quiet area for a few moments can work wonders. When the child comes out, don't refer to the past violation. Act as though it never happened. Then praise the first good thing she does.

8. Excessive use of "quiet time" or "time out" neutralizes its effectiveness. Use it sparingly, or you'll have a belligerent child on your hands who has little respect for you or herself.

9. This is important. Watch your own conduct. Your ethics must be above reproach. If you expect

your child to behave gracefully, you behave gracefully.

10. Talk about the importance of cooperation. We have to give in sometimes, bend like a willow tree or break in the storm. Cultivate a love for all humanity in your child, and "bending" will become easier for her.

The subject of handling temper tantrums needs special treatment.

Compassionate understanding should be your first consideration in dealing with your emotional child. Why is he acting up? Does he feel he needs more attention than he's been getting lately? Does he feel threatened by a sibling, your spouse, or a friend? Could he be tired or hungry? Children "run down" much more quickly than adults do. Or maybe he's trying to cope with a stress he is unable to talk about.

The first step is to get him off in a private area, if possible, and question him about what's bothering him.

Step two, and this takes patience, is to be understanding and reassure him of your love and support.

Finally, firmly explain expected, proper behavior —insist on it.

NON-JUDGMENT

Judging others—that is, analyzing the appearance or behavior of anyone—creates invisible, but very real walls around us and slows spiritual growth. All the effects of positive thinking, proper diet, years of meditation and spiritual study are neutralized when judgments and comparisons are made about our fellow man.

After all, who is experiencing those judgmental thoughts? You are, of course! You're the one who feels the anxiety over what someone has said or the nonverbal criticism you're thinking about the rude stranger at the store.

Therefore, whether you're out in public or just around the house, discourage critical remarks and comments about others by saying something such as "Your Heavenly Father's love flows through her, too;" or "That person is a part of you—the divine you, but he is free to do what he thinks is right."

The choice is clear. See the differences or see the Oneness! Your choice determines your mastery over the confines of this dimension and the courage you bring to life. Think petty or think big. Your children will feel your thoughts and will mimic your consciousness.

It's easy to get emotionally caught up with confrontations with friends and relatives, money problems, even global instability. In dealing with life's irritations or problems, many metaphysical/ spiritual paths teach putting "white light" around oneself or doing special chants for protection. There really is no need for this. First of all, this implies that we are better than "something out there," when we are all actually expressions of the Divine. Secondly, we get the feeling that we need protection *from* something sinister, which only promotes fear and insecurity. It gives so-called evil credibility— therefore, power!

There is no evil, only our lack of awareness of the

divine nature of all things. Force fields of protection reinforce *duality* and *separation*, clouding one's vision of the reality of Oneness. We don't need protection from anything, since we are One *with* everything. Teach your child relaxed confidence, harmony, and a love and identity with all of life. As the saying goes, "There is not a spot where God is not!" This is a much higher and clearer level of experience.

You and your child's ability to flow effectively and gracefully with the pressures of life depends primarily on one thing—spiritual stamina. Develop this through continuous realization of your identity as soul.

As John Burroughs said, "One of the hardest lessons we have to learn in this life, and one that many persons never learn, is to see the Divine, the celestial, the pure in the common, the near at hand—to see that heaven lies about us here in this world."

CHAPTER 8

Yoga and Meditation

YOGIC APPROACH TO ONENESS

Everything else in your child's world may be changing, churning, turning upside down. But she can experience life in the "eye of the tornado," the inner calm through which she can develop a true feeling of security. Some kind of daily practice, getting in touch with the higher Self, helps all young people to make an easier transition into the teen years—those years when the glands are secreting new hormones, and emotions are often on edge. Working constructively with creative energy channels it to a higher expression.

The yogic disciplines teach this truth. As the graceful asanas (postures) are assumed, the student learns to apply this exercise technique toward his daily attitude. The confident, controlled, flowing movements become a blueprint to follow in other areas of activity. When a difficult posture is encountered, the student learns to master an attitude of neutrality. In this non-resistent frame of mind, the aspiring yogi is able to put aside the temporary discomfort of the body.

Ask your child if he's noticed how difficult it is to run or move quickly in water. The resistance is very strong and he can easily get worn down as a result of his own exertion. The water doesn't *do* anything; it's the way *he interacts* with it that creates the experience. It is much easier to move in the water when adapting to it, merging with it.

It is never the circumstances outside of ourselves that need changing, but our approach or attitude toward them.

Through adopting this compliant skill, anyone can face life's challenging situations in the same manner—with grace and mastery.

You can help your child minimize stress through developing a yogic approach, especially in dealing with interpersonal relationships. Help your child cultivate the habit of looking at others and feeling a One-ness, a sameness. Tell your young person, "All of us—all of these people, and you and I, are like leaves on a gigantic tree. Some are still little tiny buds, not yet fully unfolded. But one day they will be!" As a divine helper, your child can shine a light of love on these other "leaves."

CENTERING

The importance of meditation in the daily routine for anyone cannot be overemphasized. Not only is it physically healing, it promotes an objective, rational attitude and a serenity that comes with practicing the presence of the Cosmic Life Force.

Children especially need this. In many other countries it is not unusual for children to sit in meditation for several hours at a time. Their discipline, maturity level, and respect for all life is commendable. Your child can achieve this also. These qualities can be cultivated with practice.

In explaining to your child the concept of mental

discipline, you might want to use this illustration. Tell your young person that sometimes the mind is like a wild little dog, who wants to think about all kinds of other things. But, tell him, "you are the boss. So when you're trying to meditate, you keep that little dog on the path. Pull his leash and bring him back. Don't get angry with him; he is just a sweet little dog, who doesn't know any better. Just remember, *you* are the boss and you need to keep your attention on the path!"

YOGA/MEDITATION SETS

Children can get very keyed up and jittery from the daily stimuli they are exposed to. The most worthwhile investment you can make for their peace of mind and spirit is to set aside some time daily, guiding your child to reach inward. He is then able to experience his own wisdom and self-control.

Some simple breathing exercises, followed with some yoga and a few minutes of meditation (preferably before bedtime) will not only facilitate a deep, rejuvenating sleep, but also will create a pivotal point in his life.

Fifteen minutes to a half-hour total time (10 to 15 minutes of yoga, 5 to 15 minutes of meditation, depending on age) to start is plenty for new students and very young children. Of course, this time can be extended, relative to the student.

The following are some suggested routines and pointers on getting started with regular yoga and meditation practice.

First of all, you need to establish a routine of ritual for your yoga time. This helps train the mind to be receptive and disciplined. Select the same quiet time and place daily. Have your young person use a favorite towel or blanket to sit on. A lit candle and some incense create a cozy mood.

Before beginning, sit crosslegged with the hands in prayer pose at the center of the chest. Inhaling deeply, chant slowly a few times, together, a mantra (or phrase) that connects your thoughts with the Infinite, such as OM (a Sanskrit word meaning *God*), or saying, "God and me, me and God; all are One," or simply *I AM*, which affirms the unlimited essence of your Being. The purpose of the opening chant is to draw attention in from the outside world and focus it on the eternal nature.

Closing the eyes during yoga, and especially during meditation, helps keep attention centered on the inner experience. This may be difficult for new

Prayer Pose/Tuning in

students or very young children. Often it feels awkward to have our eyes closed in normal waking hours. Gentle and continuous reminders help to achieve this discipline.

Be tolerant of your student's beginning efforts. Children will naturally be fidgety, so keep it short and light in the beginning. It should be a happy experience.

Follow this opening chant with a few minutes of long, deep breathing: inhale, relaxing the abdomen and filling the lungs to capacity; then exhale, pulling the stomach in and squeezing all the stale air out. Make the breaths as long and slow and deep as possible. This soothes the nervous system, oxygenizes the blood, expands the lung capacity and aids circulation. Most importantly, correct breathing helps to slow the continuous inner dialogue or chat-

Deep Breathing

tering of the mind. Stilling of the mind is the first step toward disciplined meditation.

Here are a few easy yogic exercise sets to practice regularly. They are simple to remember and quite effective in reducing stress. Do one set a day and alternate them. Remember, when doing yoga, to move gracefully and consciously. Rest briefly after each posture.

Yoga Set #1

Begin with a short chant and a few moments of deep breathing.

A. *Arms Up*. After a few moments of ''centering,'' sit crosslegged, raise the arms up at a 60° angle, palms up as if trying to hold up the ceiling. Hold

Arms Up

this posture while breathing slowly and deeply. For children, begin with half a minute to a minute. Then relax the arms gracefully.

B. *Bottoms Up*. The next exercise releases tension that tends to build up in the lower torso, keeps the spine flexible and stimulates the thyroid gland. Lie on the back with knees propped up and apart. The arms are at the sides, touching or grabbing the ankles. Inhale, raising the buttocks up. Exhale, slowly coming down. Repeat, doing five to ten of these for children. Relax.

C. *Triangle Pose*. The third exercise stretches the life nerve in the back of the legs. It will also help your child develop patience. Begin on all fours (hands and knees) and slowly come up into a triangle shape—the legs and arms are straight. The bottom is up and the head hangs down. The feet and hands should be flat on the floor, the weight equally distributed, the knee caps relaxed. Hold this posture for a count of 10 to 20, depending on the age and condition of the student. Adults can hold the posture up to three minutes.

While holding this posture, remind the student(s) to breathe slowly and deeply, keeping the attention on the *breath* and not the body. Come out of the posture gracefully, bending the knees, then sitting on the heels. Relax.

D. *Neck Rolls*. The last exercise in this set looks easy and yet releases a great deal of tension. (Yes, children become much more tense than adults realize.) Neck rolls begin with the chin close to the

Bottoms Up

Triangle Pose

chest, rotating around to the right, making a slow (3 to 5 seconds), wide circle all the way around to the left shoulder and back down to the center of the chest. Tell children to imagine a pencil coming out of the top of their heads. They want to make as wide as possible a circle above them on the ceiling. Do this several times and reverse the direction, rotating the head to the left several times.

After your exercise set and a short rest on the back, a simple candlelight meditation has a very soothing, peaceful effect on children and adolescents. (A note on the use of candles: It should be advised that adult supervision is mandatory and that children should be reminded of the importance of fire safety.)

Neck Rolls

Candlelight Meditation

Place a lit candle two to four feet from your child and you, or at the center of a group. Ask her to relax and gaze at the candle. Guide her to begin long, deep breathing. As she is doing so, direct her attention to observing the candle, noting all its attributes; the color, the shape and movements of the flame, the glow of the light, the scent (if any). Ask her to imagine that nothing else exists besides this candle. After a moment of two, ask her to close her eyes and

Candlelight Meditation

''see'' the candle in her mind. Finally, after a moment or so, ask her to imagine that she and the candle are one, that she *is* the candle.

This meditation exercise is a spiritual/emotional/ mental discipline. It strengthens inner security, concentration, imagination, intuition, and spiritual expansiveness.

Tell your child soothing, positive words of inspiration as she is going into the meditation. ''You are a light in the world. Wherever you go, you spread light, love and understanding. Your light is a light of healing, growth and freedom. You are a star in the heavens.''

Close your yoga session with the hands in prayer pose once again. Ask your child to think of someone who is sick or upset or having a problem, and imag-

Imagine someone you know as radiant, happy and free!

ine that person being *perfect, radiant* and *free*. This cultivates generosity and compassion for human suffering.

Yoga Set #2

Begin with a short chant and a few moments of deep breathing or alternate-nostril breathing.

Alternate-nostril breathing is done with the right hand brought up alongside the right nostril, the thumb applying slight pressure to close the right nostril. Inhale deeply through the left nostril, using the same hand, then switch over and block off the left nostril with the little finger and exhale through the right. Then inhale right, exhale left. Change sides only after each inhale. Keep the breath long, slow and deep. This breath balances the positive,

Alternate-Nostril Breathing (Inhale left)

negative (or introvert, extrovert) energy flow in the aura and is a good breath to practice before an important discussion or presentation.

A. *Rag-Doll Bend*. Ask your student to stand erect with arms stretched overhead to the ceiling, then slowly bend at the waist, letting the upper torso drop; shoulders, arms, everything should be limp. But don't let the knees bend too much. Then— slowly stand up. Vary your time according to the age.

B. *Side Bends*. Stand with the feet apart about a foot, and bend sideways from the waist, sliding the left arm down the side and extending the right arm straight up. Hold the pose for a count of five and slowly change sides.

Alternate-Nostril Breathing (Exhale right)

Rag-Doll Bend

Side Bends

C. *Cow-Cat Pose*. Come down on all fours (hands and knees) and ask your child to lift the head up as if looking at the ceiling. This is the cow pose. Inhale as the head is lifted up. Then on the exhale, bring the chin down on the chest and arch the back up like a cat. Do this several times, alternating cow, cat, inhaling, exhaling. This loosens the spine. Then relax on the stomach.

D. *Cobra Pose*. To do the Cobra (snake), lie down on the stomach with the legs together and the hands flat down on the floor by the shoulders. Slowly raise the head up to look at the ceiling, bringing the shoulders and chest up—straighten the arms and hold for a count of five to ten for children (3 minutes maximum for adults). Slowly come down, being careful to keep the head up until the very last. Relax on the stomach with the arms at the sides.

Rainbow Meditation

Talk to your young person about rainbows. After the great flood, Noah's ark came to rest after a long time, and a beautiful rainbow appeared in the sky as a sign from God that he loved us.

Sit straight in an easy pose and imagine a beautiful rainbow inside the stomach, stretching up to the throat, up through the top of the head to a radiant, sparkling star above the head. Hold this thought and feel healthy, wise and happy.

Close as always with the hands in prayer pose.

Cow-Cat Pose

Cobra Pose

Yoga Set #3

As always, begin with a short chant and deep yogic breathing or alternate-nostril breathing.

A. *Lion's Roar*. This first exercise tones the face muscles and releases tension and frustrated emotions. Sit on the heels and put the hands on the floor in front. Inhale and roar—stretching the tongue out and widening the eyes like a lion. This is a favorite with children. Do it several times and relax.

B. *Camel Ride*. Sitting in easy pose, grab the ankles with both hands. Inhale and pull forward, pushing the chest forward. Exhale and slump the back, relaxing the arms. Get a moderate rhythm going—inhaling forward, exhaling slump. This is just how riding a camel feels.

Lion's Roar

Camel Ride

C. *Rocking Horse*. To do the Rocking Horse, lie on the stomach, reach back and grab the ankles. Pull up and rock from chest to knees for a count of five to ten for children (2 minutes maximum for adults).

D. *Bridge Pose*. This is a more difficult posture. Mastering it aids in "bridging across" obstacles. Sit with the knees propped up and the arms behind, hands supporting, flat on the floor. Bring the bottom up, allowing the head to drop back. Breathe deeply and hold the posture for a count of five to ten for little ones (3 minutes maximum for adults). Relax slowly and lie on the back for a few minutes.

Rocking Horse

Bridge Pose

Lotus Meditation

Tell your young person to draw all thoughts in, away from the world. Take a few minutes to breathe deeply and become aware of the body sitting there. Tell your child, "Imagine the heart and how it beats, sending life through the body. Imagine a beautiful blue ball of light where your heart is. See it grow. After a moment, imagine it changing into a beautiful lotus flower. See it open up, petal by petal. A wonderful fragrance fills the room. The center of the flower is so bright! There is someone in the

Prayer Pose

middle of the lotus flower. Look closely and you will see your spiritual Master (Jesus, Krishna, Yogananda, Sai Baba, a teacher or an angel) smiling lovingly at you." Hold the vision for just a few moments, not so long that it gets boring.

Relax for a moment and close with the hands in prayer pose.

Practicing yoga, meditation or simply casual daily conversations about values helps your child keep an obective perspective in life, increases his self-confidence and keeps him centered. A centered child is more receptive to a greater flow of creativity.

Daily spiritual sessions strengthen your bond with him. And where there is a spiritual-love bond, there is heaven on earth!

CHAPTER 9

The Highest Goal

The first duty to children is to make them happy. If you have not made them so, you have wronged them. No other good they may get can make up for that.

Buxton

Making children happy does not refer to giving them everything their little hearts desire. Frequently, beyond the temporary thrill, this makes them quite unhappy.

The joy of childhood is the joy of life itself! Indulge them in the whimsical world of life beyond the physical, the realms of fantasy.

IMAGINATION

Imagination has been called "the eye of God," the "Divine dream," the "essence of Reality," and other descriptive euphemisms. In addition to all these, imagination is the life breath of children, the heart of their very existence.

Adult skepticism and logic do more damage to a child's inquisitive, creative spirit than any one other single factor in this world, including television. When your child relates his point of view, or experiences he's had—no matter how outlandish they may seem—don't critize, ignore, or laugh at him.

Your child is keenly aware on all levels: emotionally, intellectually, psychically and spiritually. Keep in mind that he may be able to see into other worlds, other dimensions (whose validity is being increasingly acknowledged by parapsychologists in their research), when he comments that he's seen lavender trees before. A good response would be, "That's possible," or "I see it differently, but what you see is real, too." Always build his confidence and his creativity through giving him credit on his imagination.

DREAMS

In many cultures of the world (generally called *primitive* by our standards) where disease is unheard of and the natives exhibit a high degree of mental calmness and serenity, the reality of dreams and the sharing of them is an integral part of the day.

Dreamers share, at breakfast time, their nocturnal experiences, working out with the conscious mind what they "lived" in the subconscious. In this healthy manner, inner conflicts are brought to light, precognitive talents are increased, and an intuitive bond between group members is strengthened.

Disruptive dreams are talked over, and the dreamer is encouraged to make up his own happy ending, thus resolving any upsetting psychological feelings.

All dreams are a level of reality—whether they are the momentary reveries that break up daytime activities or night-time experiences. These events are truly happening on some level of the being.

What criteria determines what is real and what is not? How often are daily schedules and duties performed mechanically in a nearly unconscious state? By comparison, a vivid dream, bursting with color and excitement, adventure and enthusiasm, would be more real in terms of awareness. A dream such as this exhibits the primary ingredient of reality itself: vitality!

Where the awareness is—there the consciousness is. And where the consciousness is—there is the reality. Even during daydreams we are not really "here," but "somewhere else," though our body continues to function automatically.

Adults often wonder if encouraging the fantasies and dreams of children invites disassociation from the real world. If your child is taught how the physical and nonphysical levels of learning interconnect, this worry becomes needless. Everything is a part of everything else. Matter is just condensed spirit.

Encourage breakfast "dream time." It's healthy!

WORKING WITH BECOMING THE POWER AND PRESENCE

All life, all experiences, are real in varying degrees of divinity. And all of life vibrates from the invisible to the visible—ideas moving into form—imagining something with enthusiasm and then experiencing it. This is a holistic and therefore truly spiritual approach to living. And it is a spiritual milestone for anyone, child or adult, to realize—not intellectually, but on a deep *feeling* level—that everyone and everything is an expression of the Creator, in different stages of awakening.

Your child's realization that he is an expression of the Source is like turning the doorknob. Opening the door is the next step. Once he establishes in his awareness the capacities of his divinely creative identity, your child can have the joy of experiencing the flow of spiritual energy rushing through him, and can then consciously direct that energy by using the talents he is best suited for, to find fulfillment according to his individuality. This is the beautifully reciprocal and harmonious operation of "surrender" and "free will."

Your child's mastery of Life will be determined by the degree to which he is harmonizing with the Infinite. The acute consciousness of who he really is—a divine expression of the Creator—is the pinnacle of true success.